Sprint Cars

BY DENNY VON FINN

BELLWETHER MEDIA • MINNEAPOLIS, MN

™

Are you ready to take it to the extreme?
Torque books thrust you into the action-packed worl
of sports, vehicles, and adventure. These books ma
include dirt, smoke, fire, and dangerous stunts.

WARNING: READ AT YOUR OWN RISK.

This edition first published in 2009 by Bellwether Media, Inc.

No part of this publication may be reproduced in whole or in part without written permission of the publisher. For information regarding permission, write to Bellwether Media, Inc., Attention: Permissions Department, Post Office Box 19349, Minneapolis, MN 55419.

Library of Congress Cataloging-in-Publication Data
Von Finn, Denny.
  Sprint cars / by Denny Von Finn.
    p. cm. — (Torque. Cool rides)
  Includes bibliographical references and index.
  Summary: "Full color photography accompanies engaging information about sprint cars. The combination of high-interest subject matter and light text is intended for students in grades 3 through 7"—Provided by publisher.
  ISBN-13: 978-1-60014-257-4 (hardcover : alk. paper)
  ISBN-10: 1-60014-257-5 (hardcover : alk. paper)
  1. Sprint cars—Juvenile literature. I. Title.

TL236.27.V66 2009
  629.228—dc22   2008035638

Contents

What Is a Sprint Car?

Sprint cars are built for speed. A sprint car weighs around 1,200 pounds (540 kilograms). A normal car is almost three times as heavy! Sprint cars have powerful engines with a lot of **horsepower**. A light car with a powerful engine has a good **power-to-weight ratio**. This helps make the car faster. Sprint cars can reach speeds of 140 miles (230 kilometers) per hour!

Fast FaCt

Sprint car engines create more than 800 horsepower. That's almost four times as much as a normal car engine.

Sprint car races are very intense. The word "sprint" means a short race. Sprint cars race less than 40 miles (64 kilometers) per race. Several cars race at high speeds on a small **circle track**. The combination of fast speeds, small tracks, and many cars makes crashes common during sprint car races.

Sprint Car History

Early auto racers competed at dirt tracks all over the United States. Most early race cars were large and expensive. In the 1950s, race cars became smaller and more affordable. More drivers were able to race because of the lower cost. The sprint car was one of these smaller race cars.

Fast FaCt

Top NASCAR drivers such as Jeff Gordon, Kasey Kahne, and Tony Stewart drove sprint cars at one time.

Sprint car racing became very popular because races were held in small towns outside of big cities. Today, World of Outlaws is the most popular sprint car series. These cars still race in small towns across the United States.

Parts of a Sprint Car

Most sprint cars have two **wings** to help stabilize the car. One wing is on the roof. The other wing is on the hood. Air rushes over the wings during a race. The rushing air pushes the car down, keeping the car on the track. Racers call this **downforce**.

Sprint car engines are extremely powerful. The **fuel-injected** engine sits right in front of the driver. These engines have eight **cylinders** that burn **methanol** instead of gasoline to generate more horsepower.

wing

wing

Sprint car drivers must be protected during crashes. A driver is protected by a **roll cage**. These strong metal bars surround the **cockpit**. They shield the driver if the car rolls over.

A sprint car's tires are not all the same size.
The right tires are larger than the left tires.
This is called **stagger**. Sprint cars race on oval-
shaped tracks. This means drivers only turn left
during a race. Stagger helps the driver turn more
easily because one side of the car weighs more
than the other.

Sprint Cars in Action

Sprint car engines cannot start on their own. The cars must be started with the help of **push cars**. Then the starter waves the green flag. The sprint cars are off! The push cars exit the track.

Fast FaCt
Push car drivers are often volunteers from the audience!

The engines of more than 20 sprint cars roar as they accelerate. Drivers skid around the turns on the dirt track. Dust fills the air. The track is only a quarter-mile (400 meters) around. The drivers need to complete 40 laps.

The sprint cars are wheel to wheel. The action is intense. The drivers are cramped inside their small cockpits. They accelerate through the turns. They use controls to adjust their cars' wings. They try to gain any edge they can to win the race.

Fast FaCt

Wings also act as a cushion if a sprint car flips onto its roof.

Glossary

circle track—a round or oval racetrack

cockpit—the area of a car where the driver sits

cylinder—the engine part in which fuel is burned to create power

downforce—a physical force that pushes a sprint car down on the track and helps keep it from flipping over

fuel-injected—a type of engine in which precise amounts of fuel are sprayed into the cylinders

horsepower—a unit for measuring the power of an engine

methanol—the alcohol-based fuel used to power sprint cars

power-to-weight ratio—an engine's horsepower divided by the weight of the car it powers

push cars—vehicles that help sprint cars start their engines by pushing them at the beginning of a race

roll cage—a set of strong metal bars that protects the driver if the vehicle rolls

stagger—the difference in size between the tires on the right and left side of a sprint car

wings—large, square metal panels on the roof and hood of a sprint car that create downforce

To Learn More

AT THE LIBRARY

Schaefer, A. R. *Sprint Cars*. Mankato, Minn.: Capstone, 2007.

Sexton, Susan. *Sprint Car Racing: Unleashing the Power*. Logan, Iowa: Perfection Learning, 2003.

Thompson, Luke. *Sprint Car*. Chicago, Ill.: Children's Press, 2000.

ON THE WEB

Learning more about sprint cars is as easy as 1, 2, 3.

1. Go to www.factsurfer.com.

2. Enter "sprint cars" into the search box.

3. Click the "Surf" button and you will see a list of related Web sites.

With factsurfer.com, finding more information is just a click away.

Index

The images in this book are reproduced through the courtesy of: John J. Kaliber, Jr., front cover, pp. 4-5, 8-9, 10, 12-13, 15, 19 (upper); Sports Illustrated / Getty Images, pp. 6-7; Tom Kelly / Associated Press, p. 7 (upper); Charlie Neibergall / Associated Press, p. 11; Doug Johnson, pp. 14, 16-17, 20-21; Ellis Neel / Associated Press, p. 16 (lower); Ars_1024, pp. 18-19.